EMBLEM
LUCY MERCER
MMXXII

EMBLEMATA V. CL.
ANDREAE ALCIATI
cu Imaginibus plerisque
restitutis ad mentem
Auctoris.
Adiecta compendiosa
explicatione Claudij
Minois Diuionensis,
et notulis extempora=
rijs Laurentij Pigno=
rij Patauini.

Patauij apud Pet. Paulum Tozzium. M.DCXIIX.

An emblem is a hybrid form of text and image that emerged during the early modern period. Many emblems have a three-part structure: an *inscriptio* (motto), *pictura* (picture – usually woodcuts) and *sub-scriptio* (text). But some just have two parts. Any attempt to define this protean form tends to fail spectacularly. There is no normative emblem. The relation of text to image in emblems is uneasy and arbitrary, but they also reinterpret and reinforce each other, inducing murky contemplation as we move from one part to another and back again. Another name for emblems is 'speaking pictures' as they give impossible voice to images, just like dreams. The Jesuits thought of them as having a 'soul' (text) and a 'body' (image) – though who is to say it might not be the other way around, or neither? A mother and a child? The living and the dead?

Emblems were semi-invented by the jurist and philologist Andrea Alciato (1492–1550), whose translated epigrams from the *Greek Anthology* were accidentally illustrated by the printer Heinrich Steiner with woodcuts in 1531. This snowballed into more emblems and images, and then into multiple editions of his emblem book being printed for nearly a hundred years. A muddy and generative material, emblems have a tendency to hoover up the world and spiral out into it, becoming transposed onto objects – frescos, woodwork, banners – or into other books. This book reuses 400-year-old images from the final edition of Alciato's *Emblematum liber* (1621), which had also become increasingly festooned with various commentaries, undoing the point of the contemplative work of the emblem, perhaps like this introduction.

Alciato's emblem book found me when I was pregnant with my son. This book is a result of that strange admixture, where perhaps not the historical Alciato but *My Andrea Alciato* and emblems became a way to think through the lonely hours of the early years of mother-hood. While some of the poems reuse Alciato's pictures, others are intended to be emblematic in the sense of hesitantly speaking to each other from inside the visual language of the interior, which is also an adjacent, imaginal world that comes to us.

EMBLEM

The heart has its reasons, which reason knoweth not
Pascal

Emblem

Which is to say about being encountered by a book – an obscure
cloud which has engulfed me in its shadowy context and unreadable
language – a composite mass that scarcely resembles the author's
intention – iridised by light, moths, woodworm and bacteria eating
– raining remade pictures and scattering its reprints – meanings
running like deer into the grey shadow of a wood – like a string I
pull it this way – like how wax melts into the gizzard of a turkey
– alarming and brightly strange – or the near-fluorescent fractals
of a complicated Romanesco broccoli that contains small amounts
of cyanide – or something so amorphous it is like what cannot be
known – which is also what the divine would be – this lumpy ball
thrown into the future – unopenable door appearing in a wall – long
phonecall between two ghosts – are these images pillows? – are
these images mirrors? – how different my spectre looks within them
– while all around a border of tortuous scrollwork brings the inside
to the outside, this folly, fol-de-rol – *festina lente* – 'make haste
slowly' – by taking one thing and putting it alongside another – stay,
invenio – you move the hand that makes this – a thing of words that
calls itself – myself –

The ball has to drop to go up
says my analyst

it is still dropping
like this book into my lap

like the image of a family
into a dark well

I am an analyst too Maryann
an interpreter of maladies

like Mary I bring them about
so I am prepared

can I believe you
little book

that the wisdom of god
is folly to us

that the fool who is silent
is no different from the wise

that what is elusive
can be caught in a leaf.

Why these images
these voices?

Why do you trouble me
branching vine?

Who can I believe?

The grass carries a sailboat
which is a quiet flower
the everlasting pea
its one-sided magenta sail
full and ballooning
as the left ventricle
in times of trouble
or this voice in my head
call it thoughtlessness
reanimation is possible
as inertia is impossible –
only smaller movements
as when a boat becomes a flower
on the patient grass.

And will you, unseen fish,
your touch still spreading
circles you cannot see –
will you show yourself
to me, if I wait here?

Dream Houses

I forget
some days
in Helepolis –
chapelles
of blue peaches
call the foam-line
'Men of Rome'
my wheel emits
uncertain as
gaspereau

Invagination

Had to make special curtains for my son's – well our – room as the window is so tall; blackout material behind falling starshapes and silver scythes; the whole fall of the curtain – I realise sitting here, waiting for my son to fall asleep – recalls the heavy drapery of that tent; before those stiff little velarii with their green and red socks drew it ópen to show her; just standing there in the shocking light of the place where there is no outside; covering and covering and covering for

Rossalia

The son turns his sleeping ear towards me
scarlet from fever,
how the thermometer's light goes
from one ear to the other blindly –
in turn, I cannot tell this face as
it appears attending, only
write as light soundlessly in the ear
seeking the structure of things without respite.
In The Palace of Dreams of the Red Siècle
crimson angels and knights doze (but oh
so cautiously) in their plush pink niches
as the conversation inside the great hall goes
anxiously on, *marmor marmor marmor* –
my son, we have given you our two
priscae gentilitatis obsoletum errorem –
two old and outmoded pagan
understandings.
And now you are asleep, I am fearfully
examining them with this little battery light –

Zero

I have undressed myself with salt –
look, a body of uninfinite holes
plunging unbearable things inside
like the patient-doctor relation.
But I always remember, Ajax.
I also remember on an empty walkway,
how she comforted her child even when
even when, even when, even when
Romanum postquam eloquium –
the fiercest are tamed. Oh landslides' line
as when you see houses turn a hill.
Nothing is clean of bringing absence,
says me, who doesn't want to give up
anything.
There is a gate from which bodies emerge
like an autopsy. I am not that gate …

Single Mother

The sea dropped its findings or unfastened
as two brief-lit hard parapets unfastened;
made a wild chronotope out of my body,
but now, *said Anne*, I am matronly,
my climaxes perverse in their free
zigzags of melted sutures, these stiff fingers,
aliens of no beginning, alone with me,
another evening in spent moving them
across my picturebooks: watching *clouds*
dream spray and spray across the silver *sss*
ssealed sea

*

Fell into the matricene *h*our problematic
ten thousand years of thorny overwhelmed
mothers flighted spinning in such spheres of fright,
mothers repeating *Polly-Polly-Poly-glot*,
mothers sealing ears with moly the plant,
mothers levering scabs on legs earliest of the sofa,
mothers plucking hairs like shot birds
preparing themselves   no eschatologies *Ω*

Single Mothers Study Metaphysics

In labour, on all fours changing
what is elsewhere for what is here
the body casts vomit onto the floor

The mind images it is drowning
eye-high muddy Ocean, two buoys
floating on the rising rows

Forever watching the cinematic
threshing-floor of its own inquisition,
this mind that is the body's idea –

Which demands a repayment
for damage done by its investment,
guttering sense with sensation

Like a candle tired of speaking,
how often now it practises disruptment
pacing and smoking around

The foxgloves purple in pieces,
sometimes folded into its knees,
for it, the mirror its only witness.

Apple

My sightless self-weaving
mother meant to show

how beautiful the trailing
light is riding back out

from her mirror of hundreds –
I, my brothers and sisters,

but what she knows and what I know?
call it the change;

what I learned as I became
knowing I shall die for
her love of light.

(I know you,
all you creatures of mouths,
what you like,

your bodies like bubbles
burst upon foam.)

so I am sending light
this way around this way

so I can show you Axis,
I know how you desire
Axis

Divination

My son has an orange cat torch he loves.
Open its mouth and a bright light comes out

The cat is surprised at this –
its satsuma voice is completely – gone?

In these grey minutes I am opening
and closing its mouth with a loud click.

Show me how you do that trick
as we have all so wanted, we have
wanted to carry out a search ...

TEXT & IMAGE

This thinking carries with it I know not what secret horror;
one finds oneself wandering in a great immensity devoid
of any limit or center, and therefore of any determinate place.
Kepler

Reading

My mind bends its face like a flower
to a lit window
as I take the thought into my mouth

And as my head grows full with it
my hearing stampedes like horses
inside
the sea floor
the wildebeests in the canyon

Past a ladder in an old painting
(almost a cartoon yellow ladder)
used by stagehands in a theatre
by leaning it against a spectacularly
closed curtain
the painter shows us how things that are veiled
cannot be reached
though we try to reach them
with hands that move to directions
not quite ours

There is no light in the window
no substance behind the hellish
weaving
no myself veiled to myself

Wandering now in a meadow
of breezeless blue
as pages turn into flowers –

As the field forgets this is the blue
laughter of forget-me-nots who do not
remember at all –

Ten Shifts

I

at sunset
take hold of a drinking-cup
with two ears

this is your head

as you know
underneath are two roses
one red and one green

whatever you do
you mustn't eat
both the roses

II

some time during this   it
wriggles away
out of the room

the moon
cross-roads

it lies in
the middle of the road with a wide open mouth, and cries,
has to confess

it had stood by your side
in the hall. then you disappeared

it had eaten you
its wide open mouth was a road
of letters

III

so, you think
so so
so, a word said by no-one

and the moon rises
and so   again
so
and so

there seems
a distant country
sleeping all alone
for you
to know

IV

lo and behold!

you want a fate

V

all I tell you
in ten shifts

and lies

you must
hold it in your arms

VI

all disappears again into the oak tree

VII

dissolving and cutting
this superstition
arrayed in the strangest robes
conducted with music
and torches
as soon as the door is shut

VIII

a shift

little eyes roll furiously afraid
and command

nothing left but a huge thick mass

dragged

IX

spinning and gurgling
the veins' wool
subject to no-one

like the sun too

as you know
it is sunrise now

X

at last you decide
on the red rose
and you eat it

at last you decide
on the green rose
and you eat it

one is called text
and the other, image.

Woodcut Print

Into is it memory we press and press
and *and* pulps like old flowers – armour?
And we press tied somehow
somehow still ourselves?

Past a spilled person resting in wet lines,
soldiers lacing swords over me, a tree.
Here I am sightless & you voiceless?
Tell me again, tell me again in the dark.

Mirror

I go deep into my instincts
But domestication pulls me back

Like the way the wind takes a line
Takes these wet t-shirts against itself –

Not that I feel it, the wind,
I just see it, like everything else.

Hydrangea: '*The Angel is in my molten blue ear…*
                 You must learn to live uneasily, Andrea.'

You cannot engrave a hydrangea, nor does it have the capacity
to bite deeply into stone (this is why ivy, the poet's flower, is flowerless).
The Lernaean Hydra *of language though, is like a stick that cuts*
with no end.

Westworld

When I hear stories of what happens to bodies
I cover the holes in my face
as my son, too, has a body –

As if I could board up the unhinged doors and windows
of this unfortunate saloon
leaving Extreme Worry out in the midday sun
crushing violets and sticking them onto cactuses
shooting deer that look like other cowboys

Who after all, learn from their mothers
a reckless love of the pursuit of death.

If I believed, I could ring up my heart's
transparent attorney and ask, please –
don't let him be horribly damaged –

There aren't any phonelines out here.
There don't seem to be any women either.

In the sunlit display of the throughway
a grocer kneels in the dirt to crack a coconut
after watching its liquid flying about
he replaces it with the others on the stack,
the top back on, not perfect, but back on
like a television showing a fire in a fireplace.

Perhaps our desire to order what breaks
is our best human feeling.

Like Picinelli who wanted to make a Book of the World,
he found a bundle that grew into a heap
then a huge shapeless mass
and felt compelled to dispose this chaos
into some ordered design.

It grows dark. Trees and streets are a grey gloop
in the window.

My son's favourite book is where you look for a man
who hides in the middle of large crowds.
We look at it again, our faces pressed close.

At first it seems he's not in the picture
and so is unlikely to be found. But he is there
and in this book each question has an answer:

'Where is ... the man in a fountain?'   'Where is
the keen barber?'   'the puncture caused by an arrow?'
'a waiter who isn't concentrating?'   'a dog on a roof?'
'a boy attacked by a plant?'   'Where is a man coming out
of a manhole?'   'Where are two firemen waving at each other?'

My son is sleeping like a peachstone.

Tonight, after walking a world, the picture man
opens his mouth for me
and I can see his throat looks the same as mine.

He says   'satisfactory questions?'   he says   'where the answer
has already been decided?'   'why are you looking
out here?'   'criminal defendants'

     he says   'history'   'not this history'
'your face'   'my face'   'no answers'   'a book but not a world'
        he says

'a world but no book'   'like mine'   'cannot imitate your face'
'what you know now'   'what does knowing do?'   'has ever done?'

'who are you looking for?'

Fragments

I

A semtex explosion of organs
whenever the grass resutures
our purple reins

II

Putting my hands over my body
I, revenant. Empty tents, the dipped
pooled rubbish moonlit in the road

A circus camped in the shape of a crosier
a snake dreaming time in looping fire –
a state before thought but no state intact

III

The decoy duck flies to the nets
she's a spinning wheel

here she comes flying to the nets
    and they follow

soon they'll be quiet as Romans
under the sun's feathers –

like opening the same door
like opening the same door

IV

The only law is the law of ornament

Chimera

In a circle, we sit and tell of things we've done
wrong. Some faces are swollen like the drowned mid-rescue,
as is mine from crying over pictures –

Speech keeps flying from one of us to another
as green hummingbirds like to dip their long beaks
right into a flower's business –

Into my sternum hiding something that quivers
like the kittens my mother was given had they been kept
in the bag and lowered into the muddy river –

What can be done, my mind asks the spirit
who brings a golden bridle into dreams
who only comes unbidden like the best and worst of things

like how proverbs appear –
The morning is wiser than the evening, says Vasilisa's little doll.

Imago

I walk up to a black bucket
full of water and full of an image,
it's a reflection again

if I could see above, it would not
startle me.

we are in an invisible harness,
Andrea,
but it's only with asymmetries

like water distorting in a bucket
like the shock of being entered by another
like a birthday that was easier last year –
that we can believe we are moving.

this is the beloved who walks around and closes
the eyes of carnations in the air.

THIS THING IS
THE CLOUD

The thought is enuoluped in obscurete & vnder the clowdes.
Caxton

Phantasias

I sense you in the dank underpass
of the live chauvette cave that rebuses
in ruches, bubbles and lumps when I
slip past the figures so unintent
on their work, past the line-ladder of study
a line-ladder of shadow where the bracket
rises untethered like me as I am here
in the poem too its rings of rock so carefully
winding through one another. It is not hard
to get here when the sun is looking hard
through any window when the ground
is moving like *so* when the rain comes
and the trees are watery reflections
little fleshy waves coaxed by the unbearable
promise of living in the world we are supposed
to know, its fatal arrogance notwithstanding.
How quickly the restraining hand appears
across my sight scribbling you away
like a child's impatience with its drawing,
not wanting to leave what it had shown.

Shadow

Opened a door onto a drawn field full of tigers that were licking
the light, but all I could think at that moment while watching them
 so orange and true was
I should like to be a drawn field ... with the sun's first joy coming
 towards me
holding my mind like a thin blue plastic kite before it's given up to
the wind, the deep spine resting between beams of light. 'Thalassa we
see you!' says the light. 'Making all the rivers so salty they cry out
 in books!'
I should like to wear a curling worm costume to struggle out of and
join the mosquitoes in their frenetic evening performance by a house
set into a marshy meadow, all deep set into its place with a wool
wheel inside with red thread wound all around it.
Something like a string of glue coming from my mouth. *iam satur
 de gramine* ...
Even the light doesn't know who I am. I take off my deepsea
underwear – and I'm just a fox holding a mask made of white clay:
restless, *Andrea*, I'm such a restless index ... *(page)*
 (every page)

(iam every page)

Chirologia

Climbing the stairs, I see no neighbours' lights
and the son is still sleeping before his first day.
There's a rainstorm outside, quieting the city.

Whatever's here is turning its face away.
Like when you anticipate a fly's path, John –
and with your hand vibrate the air,
so the fly feeling it then travels past.

I lie in my dark stage bed and remember.
I. Recommendo, one hand underneath the other;
G. Confido, one palm pressed upon another's back
both drooping down with shared knowledge;
O. Adoro, they are to the lips;

In this remembering,
the sensation of difference between hands,
two frightened butterflies, becomes unhinged.

O carpenters, like the window against the wind,
the language of hands is indifferent to resistance.

Follow me outside the open gate
the sky is sleeping fringed and rose
like a candle in the dark marsh.
The gate is   fringed candlelike in
a dark sky   sleeping and open
outside the rose marsh follow me.

Follow me outside the open gate
the sky is sleeping fringed and pink
like a candle in the rose marsh.
The gate is   fringed candlelike in
a rose sky   sleeping and open
outside the pink marsh follow me.

The gate is   fringed candlelike in
the sky sleeping fringed and pink
outside in the pink marsh follow me.
Follow me outside the open gate
a rose sky   sleeping and open
like a candle in the rose marsh.

Gelassenheit Bath

Have I told you about the war I was in? It was so long, I cannot
remember if it was a war at all. Long as my legs sleeping under the
glassbathwater: long as a beach of ruffled woodwork bathing a red
skeleton with a sword stuck in his making parts.

My back is covered with thousands of tiny bubbles I have been in this
bath such a long time. I move it gently back and forth against paint
dense as miles-down grains of sand.

Above, a terrible sun distorts the way form condenses the shapes
of dreams. Trailing festoons of light plunge down towards me, a seal
– a hermaphroditic woodcut cephalophore with a crown of daffodils
on its missing head swimming the world limit.

And this razor here cuts underneath my arm like young grass
perhaps being cut if there is such a thing as young grass or like a
granite whetstone taking away the Sunday knife or like dried out
branches tapping their sighs into glass or like how the falling harvest
grew on the tablets of Assyria.
It is hard to domesticate water.

The other arm has become quite heavy; it is not mine just as this
whole body is not mine. Now it's four-o-clock on a Sunday and in the
bathroom window the sky is as radiant as a rained-on tile in the house
of *Yves* & I am afraid and look away.

Katabasis

a 'Classical' stone angel points her mould-finger to the sky ringing
its blue phones; hundreds of sweating horses with ultramarine
saddles running in a complete blur; trees break into images on the
long-collapsing stone; into images as the dead live in images only;
that are not still and do not stay; even these crosses and angels of
stone are not so rigid; as though one torso on another were the lace of
the same palm tree; though even a single grass is full of complicated
history; whose mouth is this close underneath? I'm sure their beauty
would surprise me, though I could not understand it; long gaze that
never comes back; a face like sunlight;

willow-pollen dusting the street margins into sand; the truth is I
am afraid of being left alone in pain; *I am not dead, I am half-asleep*;
I have the same hands as the statue of the angel; one day I will not
have these hands; they hold my face as I lie down on this stone that
is not a page; *I am sorry for trying to disturb you as you are not
disturbed*; now this foam is taking my hearing away; the sea always
wants the ground ahead more than the ground beneath, but the sea
finds what is possible is impossible; a woman wrapped in sparkling
blue clouds drifts into the city; *have I told you lately I love you*; it
is possible; each plot rises like hundreds of floating green sandals
of grass; if I could walk with them I would not be coming back; but
I never comes back –

Mentem, non formam plus pollere.

Ingreſſa vulpes in Choragi pergulam,
Fabrè expolitum inuenit humanum caput,
Sic eleganter fabricatum, vt ſpiritus
Solùm deeſſet, cæteris viuiſceret.
Id illa cùm ſumpſiſſet in manus, ait:
Hoc quale caput eſt, ſed cerebrum non habet.

'A fox, entering the store-room of a theatrical producer, found an actor's mask, skilfully shaped, so finely fashioned that the spirit alone was missing, in all else it seemed alive. Taking it up, the fox addressed it – What a head is this, but it has no brain!'

Gilgamesh's Dream

[...]

Now I'm awake, I want to tell you
like a child hovering [alert] before the darkness.
You aren't really here, no matter.
[you] only repeat names back to me –
often your own. [... double all you see.]

You might say *where is my son*, tell me again
so mother, here's a second dream –

In the square of our holiday town – Carcassonne? –
an axe was lying with crowds around it
so big they brimmed like curious clouds around it
[saying nothing ...] the axe sent sunlight spinning.

The cypress trees on the hillsides shied away
I saw the roundabout plants and animals run away.
Was it [an axe] at all? With strength only dreams possess
[I lifted it and ...] [held it] to my chest
it moved [in and out of] my skin like breath.

Situations

Earthquakes last night; from within a domed church, and a
supermarket dash to gather supplies, did not hesitate to raid the
hundreds of lobsters in their tanks and bash a few against a wall
and take them too; I was disgusted by my actions but

*

An old woman with a very long nose is dragging a sack full of kittens
in a desultory manner along the ground; I have decided to create
a live performance of Athanasius Kircher's cat piano and am taking
the kittens to pasture among the keys.

Icarus

I've come to see someone about a thing.
Its surface is separated in waves like the ribs
of wild boar roasted by the fires of men.

This thing is suspended and silent.
The unnoticed garden, the kitchen blind lit peach
with indoorsness this mid-afternoon in winter

Like a pair of lungs that had been flying
towards the outside coughing hard and dry,
a child's cough. But then had stopped.

Inhale, it would say, if it had a voice.
Just inhale the air as if you are also a fire.

Silence

Things I've seen recently about:
A solitary tree in a storm.
A Late Carolingian ivory
Where snakes corkscrew like cooked pasta up
To human feet, blank saints leave their tombs.
A green river bent into the sky
Chasing a cloud of auburn hair,
Seven flimsy foil-veined angels
Shoot useless arrows into it –
(The auburn cloud) – green river eats sky.
Your face, John, your beautiful face.

NOTATION

obscūrus
cūlus
cutis
scēo
scúwa
oscurare
obscuara
chiaroscuro

To Lullabies

I know now, my life understood
as a barless music of pressures,

that reflection is composition:
my twin daughters

when they were born
felt light as sprains in both arms.

   *

And now:

memorandums spilling onto the floor
it's mother goose coming down the stairs,

cards made for a game I have forgotten
why or for whom I am playing

the rain shakes the sky with its falling lines
like our endless requests, maman.

   *

What parsley in a washed jam jar
is foolish enough to lean out like a crowd

waving their parsley green handkerchiefs
to an invisible spectacle passing by ...

this spectacle, surprisingly,
is not a celebration –

   *

Say:

take these hands,
take these hands, the hands of a mother,
take my strength away from me,

take me on credit,
take me with you –

like greenness; sense
only comes after
these hands are given over –

Begonia Song

Open

This is her green cloak that had white arrows spilled on it
And this is the dry black soil of her working boots
This is her wandering eye made of hundreds of paper napkins
And this is her green hat ready for the sun
This is her thin face in repose (closer and further)
And this is her dark *green* belt. And these are her
Everyday things and the things that she's used to
And these are her muddiest dreams
Growing so hopefully in the outhouse floorboards
Writhing and moaning and pushing
And she's empty and she's also everyone
This is her body her spirit has blown
(That's just the strange way of objects)
This is her clay for making and this is water for when she's thirsty
We know nothing ever of what happens
Now we are quiet and still around her.

Cat Song

I would like a red, red, red cat
But I was given a green cat –
I don't want it any more ...

I would like a green, green, green cat
But I was given a red cat –
I don't want it any more ...

Gretchen am Spinnrade

A spinning wheel is like a rhyme, suggestive.
One of my parents secured one to
the fencewood green and soft
in, of course, the back garden.

This was, perhaps, the year
where the mystery sat
in a devout, teacherly way ...
A disappearance, a lack,
an unease? – I no longer recall.
Its reason is no longer important.

A green and soft theatrical curtain
smoothed into grey skein in a reproduction
of a painting from long ago and far away
found in a housebook.

Such backdrops hide the difficulty of showing
stories are impossible –

Think of a turning wheel
of redness that is scourged and scourging.
This is also like a dictionary or
an ordered set of fragments or
a book of sayings or proverbs or
an index: these are unexhausted.

Are lovers ever not tired?
Are mothers?
Catherine, a leaf does not try to hold up:
one might take the heart's weakness
and remain unable to bear.

Catherine,
one might not wish to find intact
the buried body, that which sat,
the chain, the order, the acceptance

Only rupture as when there is no image trapped in the
photocopier of sense, the air that was elbowed out

By the subject in time, that air
free of any spark, even of shadow –

To Music, by Franz von Schober

How often, when I have found myself
on my gravel-scabbed knees in anger,
you have turned your magic circle, like a self,
as if you were happiness's doppelgänger
from the other world

What is double-bladed: songs, swords,
our name – Franz Schobert –

Notation as Memory

Semibreve rest

Night comes to the countryside. To the water-filled slashes of mud, the unconventional bramble-brushes, the ivied hawthorns caught in the hedges breathing out and leaning out into the air like smokers, hidden and furious. She comes so we might know something of her daughter the day, who is so silent while performing her activity. Now all things are melting into each other's arms. No sight but dark leaves' sight, stretching net, raindrop full invisible and still. This is why a rest in music is a dark dash – before the clear melody comes back, as she always does, like the dreaded crunching of a car lighting its way down a gravel drive at its regular time; like wanting;

*

Stave

What an image of images my last hair is? Like an empty field of long grass on a winter's morning silvered by hundreds of tiny ice droplets mirroring and mirroring. It is the tide come in across the hospice pillow, like a woodcut picture of a sea where the mercury crests are caught falling, though of course they never can be. I have seen this hair before, in a dream, and I know the startling feeling of my trainers getting soaked with its coldness. If you look very, very closely at a patch of it rolling and knotted in itself, you will see five regular lines which are just five leaves of grass winding in one continuous strand; the winding face of a staff, which is a caduceus, held by a messenger wearing nothing but a hat made of a single flower to keep off the sun. As he walks his footsteps are turned in sheets by the earth's deep orchestra playing a work of love, a quick movement of forgetting.

*

Semibreve

My childhood pillowcase with cartoon stars and clouds drying on
the back of a chair? And the light shining through the cotton like the
ladder in a Piero della Francesca painting leading to a closed curtain,
always in a closed theatre? That cannot be opened or passed? And
the whole indefinable quality of thinking that comes from feeling?
How sentimentality plumps the nose? Capillaries inflamed like when
grassy seed dust in a gold field raised my back in red lashes? And
replica sheep all over the hills with their bells? The metal stamens
clanking like tongues? In the language of the heart in distress that
time can never be taken back, returned? As simple as that?

Baby Alphabet: Mother Alphabet

Here is a happy Meerkat jumping out from its hole
Here is the mazy violence of Mind

Here is a pleasant Otter playing in a blue pool
Here is the orchid drifting down to us so Open

Here is a slow Triceratops stewing leaves for supper
Here is the tablet of vision our visor of Tiredness

Here is a festive Hare frosted with shining foil
Here is the hand of letters in a Hurry

Here is a baby Earthworm sleeping in its bed
How early is the softburn shock of Evergreen

Here is a mischievous Rabbit dancing on the moon
Here is the Redness that brings greenness.

NEVER STOPS
BUSILY PLAITING
ROPES
FROM BROOM

To map thoughts like the stars in the early modern sky,
asterisks hovering like potentially poisonous anemones
in their soft clouds

*

Keep your hands under the clouds, for if you touch them
you will experience deep disappointment
as they move away from you disgusted

*

*

Why have you raised this paper shield so
close to your face, little soul?

*

*

*

In Gozzoli's frozen fresco a determined procession
is leaving Freud's Rome of dreams through the
silent openings of olive, pine and ash trees, all
hemmed in by an ornamental ivory-tight column
freeze. Nobody's saying anything. Among the
cardinals in their serious red, there's a young woman
– or young man – with wavy ginger hair, wearing a
dirty mustard smock with dead palm leaves sewn
into her hat.

She's clinging to a boy with a red cap, but his gown
has faded away to pink flesh. Two angry soldiers
with wide-brimmed but ominous metal hats are
watching them ... The painter Gozzoli himself is on
the right, his arms wrapping the air as if he's holding
a missing child, or is he practising the problem of
sculpture.

She's clinging onto her horse just like ice inlets
painted onto grass, or like a hare (depression dust-
bowl fur, wild-night eyes!) tethered to the grass
among the broom flowers, or like round oranges
holding onto stiff castelvetrano-green-leafed
branches. You can't see what her hands are holding
onto, what horse she is riding (is it a horse at all? ...)
(is it frightened? ...) (is it a difference engine,
covered with a suede cloth that looks like a rump?)

A Family of Water

Frigida Pugnabunt Calidis –
the heart is so close, so warm,
but the heart is also a pail or firebucket
that floods the cartoon fire station
as soon as the temperature rises

In this way, coldness is always a return
as hopeful as it is self-seeding

How coldly a wife might feel –

*

When the jets come
we stand next to each other
and play at being fountains
for a while

My daughter reaches upwards as if searching
for turtles nearly falling from a basin –

Though trapped by fallen rocks
our neighbour seems ready to spurt a plume
metres and metres high

Here I am, basin of printemps
partially restored –
flowers of water hiding the legs

*

And then we're just
three statues
on a fountain
that carries
a world

each seemingly
the same
as the other
the water like liquid
wax shining in the light
as continuously new
as the night also is
unfolding outside
it does not wait

Of Reluctant Interests

of myself, of fear,
of skyscrapers leading deer,
of wool, of tempo,
of the scissor that cuts the wool,
of dried-out seed trays,
of tasers, lasers, elevators,
of the poem making its logic, *it whispering of*
  the readiness of curtains,
of exposure in the pocket light,
of expression in the public light,
of usury, of use,
of the step into a life,
of filled baskets,
of marqyetry. Of end.

Apples

Parents' fear of traumatising children
is, you understand,
a fear of the knowing subject –

Like a plastic hummingbird iridescent
against a bathroom window
of slow-moving glass

Spread immobile like a sightless angel
waiting for instructions

Like a giant suspended in its tracks
by a hand of glass –

lead us not
lead us not
lead us not
lead us not

Mother

You find me wherever I go

the farther I go
the more you follow

now it is me chasing you
corroding shimmering

old complex overlooking the blue pool
in the Florida of myself

brutalist older hen pecking
at my future
turning seeds into bread
Not I
Not I

I'm out here in the coop of our history

your red historic feathers
coming out of my body
in histrionics
covering my eyes
    and my other eyes
        and my mother's eyes

Cupid's Emblems
after Andrea Alciato

In the typhoon of love's fire Cupid snaps
the lightning bolt in two like breadsticks.

*

Cupid saw a flock of birds shivering in soft shapes
& said "O fly over here sweet clouds!"
But they were bees & stung her fingers to a red glaze.

*

"Who is Cupid?"
"He's naked and small." "He carries darts."
"He's winged and wears sunglasses."
"No! Look at your pomegranates and your shields,
Your satsumas and umbrellas blown around in
The winter wind & try again ..."
"Hello?" "Hello?"

*

A flood carries two jugs along in a looping wave:
One is metal, one is clay.

METAL JUG: "Oh come closer, so we might rush through
this watery racecourse like champion horses!"

CLAY JUG: "We are neighbours, it is true,
But you will smash me up wearing your silver ribbons."

*

Walk lightly and say little, as Nemesis follows
the footprints of men.

Red or Green

I used to think the eye test question
which is brighter, the red or the green?
was a philosophical one –
though I did not know the words
philosophy or
ophthalmology.

Now I can say it like this
I thought it was not a question of subjectivity
but of objectivity –
which one was intrinsically brighter?
Finally, I was being asked what I felt
to be true.

I used to flip unsurely between them
red or green
as if determining their ripenesses
without my 'good' plaster-covered eye
with its quaint stickers of families of
zebras
gambolling right over the hole.

A difficult question –

Which is brighter, the red or the green?

I don't know
I still don't know

　　*

The green sponge in the basket poking out
like a pack of cards that play only green

The serrated green leaves of the houseplant
falling like a fountain that's not for drinking

The red towel that was made for redness
red clot gut ooze night vision

How it   rose
how it

EMBLEMATA

Obscurity

Poetry: she moves like ivy
every word re-encoding itself even after
the hostile earth dry as paper
becomes uncontrollable ivy

Unclear

Where can the eye open without memory?
Where is the squat grey octagon church?
The garage? The shop, its glittering repeating floor?
And a girl running down a drive
to a house?

As We Sit in the Dark

Over sewer-silvery seawaters
the decapitations of the past
are watched by pink campions
two birds loop like a medallion

This Thing is the Cloud

It can:
do nothing / become a flower
interleave or wait self-enclosed
die and disappear

A Huge Shapeless Mass

The aggressive tidal hand of Neptune
once bathed me, a light young eel,
you unfavoured are not safe, here
with no choice I was cast, here

Hidden

Even as a boat
mountainous fir   how can you bear
these sharp Atlantic gyres
after bringing your stiff fingers to your face
so often?

Unafraid like a star to just keep existing?

Reserved

And the quince is COTONEA
while waiting for her he takes two bites
the first whole green sphere of it
in his mouth is so sweet he takes two bites

Indistinct

What must I do
I ask the carrying grass

as if living were
not predicated upon pain

my soul might know
but we have never spoken

nor the fruit above me
and outside me
and grown out of me

Obscurity

When my son laughs, his face like the many
star-buds of the Hoya wax flower
suffuses together in a shining epicentre.
We, pleased with our walking, walk the bends,
my tracksuited body looming like a giant stem –

Unclear

Children's sentimentality
is strange and unaccountable.
All things love the consistency
of mirrors, except all the dead.
If there are gods, they must spend hours
in lukewarm swimming pools
remembering too, how things
matched

All houses thankful in retreat

As We Sit in the Dark

Was given a garland of grama grass,
lark, use this folded grama to shelter your chicks,
like these purple bells of foxgloves
dried into slips of circles like bruises,
seeking wind, do not vex us with your branches –

Eurus (the east wind) comes down to touch
a little brown-and-red kite having eaten so much –
'O mother, my guts are spilling out of my mouth'

This Thing is the Cloud

Have seen Attis holding his bloodied surgeon's hand to his lips
and laurel leaves glossy with blood in a reel
nightsearch that cuts like wine
how it shines in a cup

A flashlight goes into the mahogany and they throw up their hands
moving remnants remnants no longer
a leg, a hand, a face, a face,
this is some of the inlay I have seen

A Huge Shapeless Mass

He cannot see the gold ceiling of space
which is a relational frame

Where they cut the pupils
from the sclera soft like sudocrem

And now this face who is known
feels the unseen upon it like a son –

Hidden

Her body is like an anaconda which
is to say it is stitched together with
looped endings that send hills
slithering into their mists just as
knots of wood are taken by the
anxious planer to delineate
the cutting of boards

Reserved

EXIGEZ LA BRILLANTINE
'FORVIL'
LA PLUS
BRILLANTE
BRILLIANTINE

Indistinct

I Dim the Lights

human, human, what is human about me?

Some like to speak for the picture – some pretend the picture is
speaking – but a picture never has – and never will – speak – a picture
is a cultivar of image – and no image ever has – or ever will – speak
– some think images are still – but images are not still – and do not
stay – some think the mind thinks in language – but the mind only
has images to translate – some think writing is language – but writing
is just one type of picture – only the voice and the body speak in
language – like how I am speaking in this cavern now – unseen to
unheard – the body is not a picture – though the mind wishes it were
– though the body making the mind wishes it were – though the body
can make pictures – sometimes the body likes to speak for the picture
– sometimes the body pretends the picture is speaking – but speaking
is the body's only – some prefer pictures to voices – which is to say
they prefer death to life – as in the image world the dead are living
and the living are dead – and who is to say the living are living and the
dead are dead – something changing continuously always – in the vale
of obscurities all that is cleare is uncleare – if the text is the body's
idea of the mind – if the mind is the body's idea of itself – if the body
is what is not said by text – if the text is the voice of no-one – "I love
being asleep" – "and even more being made of stone" – "luckily I can't
see or hear" – "so don't wake me up!" – "ah, speak softly!" –

Andrea

Are you still there some days behind the door between us
And will I open that door one day to find you there
And hold you so close, and touch your face?

Will you find me when I am sick
When my green shadow pulls my heels back into the grass
And nothing will bring me back then, not even you?

Notes

Images

⌾ The woodcut images in this book are reproduced from the 1621 edition of Andrea Alciato's *Emblematum liber*, published by Petro Paulo Tozzi in Padua. This is the final edition of Alciato's *Emblemata* but by no means the definitive version, as new epigrams, illustrations and styles materialised across multiple editions of the book in different languages from its first printing in 1531 – an open text.

⌾ In order of appearance, emblem images are taken from the following emblems: 'PHILAUTIA' [Self-satisfaction, 69]; 'Mentem, non formam, plus pollere' [Intelligence matters, not beauty', emblem 189], taken from Alciato's *Emblemata*, published by Macé Bonhomme for Guillaume Rouille in Lyon, 1550; 'Hedera' [Ivy, emblem 204], an emblem that disappeared in the 1621 edition and taken from Alciato's *Emblemata*, published by Officina Plantiniana in Leiden, 1591. These images are reproduced with the kind permission of University of Glasgow Archives & Special Collections: SM34 & SM58; 'Vigilantia & Custodia' [Vigiliance & protection, emblem 15]; 'Obnoxia infirmitas' [Weakness is vulnerable, emblem 170]; 'In momentaneam felicitatem' [Transitory success, emblem 125]; 'In eum, qui truculentia suorum perierit' [On one who perished through the savagery of his own people, emblem 167]; 'Abies' [The fir, emblem 201]; 'Cotonea' [The quince, emblem 203]; 'Ilex' [The holm-oak, emblem 205]. The final additional emblem is 'Lapsus ubi? quid feci? aut officii quid omissum est?' [Where have I transgressed? What have I committed? What thing incumbent on me has been left undone?, emblem 17]. Other images are reproduced ornaments from the *Emblematum liber*. These images are reproduced with the kind permission of the University of Glasgow Archives & Special Collections: SM1226.

⌾ Photograph of the author's back garden taken in 2016, with reference to Ian Hamilton Finlay's *Proposal for a Sundial to be Placed on Marat's House in Paris* (1988).

⌾ Watercolour sketch by Aaron Angell. An alternate poster-poem version of this collaborative image and text work was produced as a print for the show 'Aaron Angell: More Sculpture About Dogs and Shadows' exhibited at Koppe Astner, Glasgow, 2018. The image refers to the head of John the Baptist.

Text

✒ Blaise Pascal epigraph: a loose translation from *Pensées* (1670).

✒ *'Festina Lente'*: refers to the printers' mark of Aldus Manutius and an emblem by Erasmus.

✒ *'Invenio'* (Latin): I come upon, I find, I discover.

✒ Maryann: this poem is dedicated in memory to the Jungian psychoanalyst Dr Maryann Barone-Chapman.

✒ 'Dream Houses' was originally part of a sculptural work made in collaboration with Aaron Angell for his exhibition 'The Death of Robin Hood', Kelvingrove Art Gallery & Museum and Glasgow Botanic Gardens, for Glasgow International 2015.

✒ 'Helepolis': the Greek name for a movable siege tower, whilst also being a phonetic referent to hell, Helen of Troy and Heliopolis – the ancient City of the Sun.

✒ 'velarii': in the houses of wealthy Romans *velarii* were porters employed to lift the curtain at the door for visitors. They are a reference to Piero della Francesca's fresco *Madonna del Parto* (1460) and Hubert Damisch, *A Childhood Memory by Piero della*

Francesca (Stanford University Press, 2007).

⚘ 'Rossalia': the Sicilian physician Giovanni Filippo Ingrassia described scarlet fever as 'rossalia' in his *De Tumoribus praeter Naturam* (1553).

⚘ '*marmor*' (Latin): marble, also phonetically similar to armour, amour, murmur.

⚘ 'priscae Gentilitatis obsoletum errorem': line from the *Libri Carolini* (*c.* 806), a refutation of the Second Council of Nicaea, against the adoration of images. The *Libri Carolini* were not printed or promulgated until 1549 during the Protestant Reformation.

⚘ '*Romanum postquam eloquium* –/ The fiercest are tamed': takes a line from and the title of Alciato's emblem 'Etiam ferocissmos domari' [Even the fiercest are tamed, emblem 29], which refers to Cicero's death as the brutal death of eloquence.

⚘ 'We have / Wanted to carry out a search': a line taken from a translation of Simone Weil's essay 'Reflections on the Right Use of School Studies with a View to the Love of God', originally appearing in *L'Attente de Dieu* (1950).

⚘ Johannes Kepler epigraph: from *Opera Omnia*, quoted in Hubert Damisch, *A Theory of Cloud: Toward a History of Painting* (Stanford University Press, 2002), p. 163.

⚘ 'Ten Shifts': an adaptation of the folk tale of Prince Lindworm.

⚘ 'the decoy duck': refers to Alciato's emblem 'Dolus in Suos' [Treachery Against One's Own Kind, emblem 50].

⚘ Caxton epigraph: taken from William Caxton, *Game and Playe of the Chesse* (1474).

⚘ '*iam satur de gramine*' ('now you've had your fill of grass'): from the medieval song sung at the mock Mass 'Festum Asinorum', the Feast of the Ass (donkey).

⚘ 'Chirologia': title and phrases taken from John Bulwer's *Chirologia, or the Naturall Language of the Hand* (1644),
an early attempt to document hand gestures with woodcuts.

⚘ 'Gretchen am Spinnrade': title of a Franz Schubert lied, adapted from Goethe's *Faust*.

⚘ 'To Music, by Franz von Schober': an adaptation of Schober's poem 'An die musik', which Franz Schubert set to a lied with the same name. Schubert and Schober became inseparable and were referred to by their friends as Franz Schobert.

⚘ '*Frigida Pugnabunt Calidis*' ('they will fight cold with heat'): the title of an emblem in Claude Paradin's *Devises heroïques* (1551).

⚘ 'Cupid's Emblems': loose adaptations of Alciato's emblems.

⚘ 'Vis amoris' [Love's might, emblem 108]; 'Dulcia quandoque amara fieri' [Sweetness turns at times to bitterness, emblem 112]; 'In statuam Amoris' [A statue of love, emblem 114]; 'Fidei symbolum' [The symbol of good faith, emblem 9]; 'Quae supra nos, nihil ad nos' [What lies above us is none of our business, emblem 103]; 'Aliquid mali propter vicinum malum' [Misfortune caused by a bad neighbour, emblem 166]; 'Nec verbo, nec facto quemquam laedendum' [Injure no-one, either by word or deed, emblem 27].

⚘ 'The aggressive tidal hand of Neptune': this poem is an adaptation of 'In eum, qui truculentia suorum perierit' [On one who perished through the savagery of his own people, emblem 167].

⚘ 'grama grass': taken from 'Gramen' [Grass, emblem 26], which mentions this special type of grass which symbolised protection and safety.

⚘ 'O mother, my guts are spilling out of my mouth': refers to 'Malè parta malè dilabuntur' [Ill gotten, ill spent, emblem 128].

⚘ EXIGEZ LA BRILLANTINE': this text is adapted from an advert for Forvil, a popular French haircream in the 1950s. It is dedicated in memory to Andrew Serafinksi.

🖋 'Speaking Pictures': includes at its end translated fragments of Michelangelo's poetic response to Strozzi's poem about his sculpture called *Night* (1526–31).

Acknowledgements

Thanks to *The White Review*, which published a portfolio of some of these poems, and to the following publications: *Hotel, The London Magazine, Magma, Oxford Poetry, Poetry London, Poetry Review, Poetry Wales, The Rialto, Spells: 21st Century Occult Poetry* (Ignota, 2018), *Altered States* (Ignota, 2021), *I'm In The Bath On All Fours* (Well Projects, 2019) and *To Sweeten Bitter: Contemporary British Poetry in Arabic Translation* (Meskeliani Editions, 2021). 'Dream Houses' was originally part of a collaborative sculptural work with the artist Aaron Angell exhibited at Glasgow International, and 'Untitled' was printed as a collaborative poster-poem with Angell by Koppe Astner (Glasgow, 2018).

I am grateful to Professor Harriet Hawkins and Professor Jo Shapcott for their warm support and guidance during my research.

Thank you to the AHRC and the Jerwood Charitable Foundation, who facilitated the writing of this book.

Thank you to Andrew and Matthew for their brilliant work on the design of this book.

Thank you to those who helped with the poems and those who helped with everything else, my son, my love, my friends and my family and my publisher, Jess.

About the Author

Lucy Mercer's poems have been published widely in magazines and anthologies. She was awarded the inaugural White Review Poet's Prize. She recently completed a PhD in which she developed a speculative theory of emblems. She teaches creative writing at Goldsmiths.

About Prototype

Creating new possibilities in the publishing of fiction and poetry through a flexible, interdisciplinary approach and the production of unique and beautiful books.

Prototype is an independent publisher working across genres and disciplines, committed to discovering and sharing work that exists outside the mainstream. Each publication is unique in its form and presentation, and the aesthetic of each object is considered critical to its production.

Prototype strives to increase audiences for experimental writing, as the home for writers and artists whose work requires a creative vision not offered by mainstream literary publishers. In its current, evolving form, Prototype consists of 4 strands of publications:

(type 1 — poetry)
(type 2 — prose)
(type 3 — interdisciplinary projects)
(type 4 — anthologies) including an annual anthology of new work, *PROTOTYPE*.

Emblem by Lucy Mercer
Published by Prototype in 2022

Design by Matthew Stuart & Andrew Walsh-Lister (Traven T. Croves)
Typeset in Mercure by Charles Mazé, released by Abyme, London
Printed in the UK by Pureprint Group

ISBN 978-1-913513-22-1

(   ) ( )   prototype   p

(type 1 – poetry)
www.prototypepublishing.co.uk
@prototypepubs

prototype publishing
71 oriel road
london e9 5sg
uk